The Last Stand

The Last Stand

John B. Lee

First Edition

Wet Ink Books
www.WetInkBooks.com
WetInkBooks@gmail.com

The Last Stand
by John B. Lee

Cover Design – Richard M. Grove
Layout and Design – Richard M. Grove
Author Bio Pic – Richard M. Grove

Typeset in Garamond
Printed and bound in Canada
Distributed in USA by Ingram,
        – *to set up an account* – *1-800-937-0152*

Library and Archives Canada Cataloguing in Publication

Title: The last stand / John B. Lee.
Names: Lee, John B., 1951- author
Description: First edition.
Identifiers: Canadiana 20250125951 | ISBN 9781998324149 (softcover)
Subjects: LCGFT: Poetry.
Classification: LCC PS8573.E348 L37 2025 | DDC C811/.54—dc23

for generations past,

present,

and for all the generations

yet to come

"… my lands are where my dead are buried …"

Crazy Horse of the Lakota Sioux

"… Lift up now thine eyes,
and look from the place where thou art northward,
and southward, and eastward, and westward.
For all the land which thou seest,
to thee will I give it, and to thy seed for ever."

Genesis 13, xiv-xv

"When the Lord thy God shall bring thee into the land
wither thou goest to possess it,
and hath cast out many nations before thee …
and when the Lord thy God shall deliver them,
and utterly destroy them;
thou wilt make no covenant with them,
nor show any mercy unto them …"

Deuteronomy 7, i-ii

"The earth is the mother of all people,
and all people should have equal rights upon it."

Chief Joseph, Nez Perce

"We will be known forever
by the tracks we leave."

—Dakota wisdom

table of contents

The Last Stand

This selection of poems was long-listed for:
Exile Edition Gwendolyn MacEwen Poetry Award 2023
and the poem "sometimes it seems"
received an Honourable Mention in:
The Ontario Poetry Society "ultra-short poem" award

Whose Last Stand?

In the late spring of 2023, my wife and I set out by car driving west from our home overlooking the shores of Long Point Bay, here in the lakeside town of Port Dover. Our destination by way of Chicago, crossing the border at Port Huron heading west by northwest for Rapid City, South Dakota, where we would join a group of American tourists traveling two weeks by bus visiting the many points of interest including Mount Rushmore, the grave of Calamity Jane and cardsharp and famous gunslinger, Wild Bill Hickock, who held the dead man's hand. We also spent a day in open top cars rambling in the midst of bison bulls, cows and calves in the natural environs of a park where they were given sanctuary, protected by government laws. We trekked the sacred black hills, walked the badlands, and the grasslands of the west. We were entertained by singers who sang true cowboy songs, and local Lakota performers who danced traditional dances, drummed in the old way, and told stories of the culture of their people, those ancestors from whom they had descended over time. We participated in the erection of a buffalo hide tepee, and formed circles of friendship with voices raised in languages no longer spoken but by a few.

A highlight for me involved the day our bus broke down at the site of the mountain carved sculpture of the Lakota Sioux warrior Crazy Horse. We remained at the site for several extra hours, gazing up at the monumental project which we were told would not be completed in our lifetime. Being something of a companion to the stony visages of the four presidents at Mount Rushmore, I found myself feeling a far deeper communion with this come-to life artwork, this imaginative rendering of Crazy Horse, mounted on a horse, and pointing over the land in memory of his statement, "My land is where my people are buried," than I did with the far more famous sculpture at Rushmore.

Hollywood has corrupted the meaning of Mount Rushmore. Alfred Hitchcock has indelibly carved the image of Eva Marie Saint and Cary Grant grappling up the famous faces of legendary men, thereby making a spectacle of an otherwise sacred image. So too, the stone edifice of the standing stone at Devil's Tower, immortalized (or trivialized depending on your point of view) by Spielberg's film Close Encounters of the Third Kind, where pixilated Americans make mash potato replicas at their kitchen tables, and then set off on half mad dashes for the landing location of visitors from outer space. I wanted to claw back the false mask of cinematic glamour to reveal the original myth of the bear claw ascent of the rock.

And yet, we romanticize one culture and demonize another at our peril. In recent times, in my home nation of Canada, there has been an inclination to make noble the lives of original people and to disparage the lives of those who crossed the ocean to make a life in this land once called 'the new world.' In the absence of the knowledge of history, we have allowed a false narrative to be invented rushing in to replace the story no longer known. I once opined that history is the property of the educated classes. I did not mean for a moment to suggest a virtue in this. When I was a student, we studied the official story as it was written by historians with the authority of established truth. This textbook history, this history of higher learning, served us well, though it may have been in the cynical appraisal of Napoleon 'the lie agreed upon,' or in the equally cynical trope 'the biography of the winners,' it was at the very least something worth considering, if not questioning.

I humbly suggest that it is the worst kind of racism to ennoble everyone of a certain ethnic origin. If we refer to someone as an elder, thereby hinting at wisdom, I ask "have you never known an old fool?" If we suggest that there was once a paradise in the wilds of America, then what of the conflict and hatred and endless wars between the Lakota and the Crow? If we suggest that nothing good ever came of first contact, then what might we say of the Spanish horses that ran wild and were captured and thereby transformed the lives of many of the aboriginal peoples roaming the plains. If the Black Hills are the sacred home of the Lakota Sioux, then what of the people displaced by the Sioux only a few hundred years prior to the arrival of Europeans moving into the American west? Is it a crime to ask?

What might the Innuit think of the Bedouin? Invaders of the Arctic, settlers of the Negev? Well as for me, I'm just a poor boy whose intentions are good, oh Lord, oh Lord, don't let me be misunderstood.

The Last Stand

The Last Stand

for Custer
it seems there was no last stand
it was rather
a scattering of bones
like the wild and random
aftermath
of a wind-torn orchard
something
beyond the reach
of a final confusion
touching through the tantalus
of a fathomless darkness
a vaporous absence
invisible as breath
smouldering up and out of an ashy
sibilance of a drying fire
hissing in the heat
of an ever-evaporating rain
when the soul surrenders
the self
like a veil exhaled in fear
and
there was no last stand
not on this *hero's* hill
this sloping ground
where the spent spirit quivered
shivered and went still
in the reedy doldrums
of universal death

down in the gully, in
the deep ravine
they also died hiding
heaped there and squirming
like worms in moss

those broken-jawed Swedes
those shatter-skulled
bluecoats
ramming the podgy-thumbed
chambers
of hot rifles
like the blunting of keys
dulled in the rusty escutcheons
of the wrong lock
when it was midnight
in the morning
and they went blind-handed
into paradise
as it is
with bones heaved
from a root-worried grave

and but what, when
and however, who
in this foe-phantom story
where at the sorrowing
of every angel-bothered moment
in wing-dusted air
the heart breaks both ways
like water over stone
to make from the flesh
this sperm and ovum monument
drumming at fire
to put eternal fire out ...

Upon Visiting the Battlefield at Little Bighorn River

the ghosts of fallen soldiers
remain
as white markers
milkening the swells and hollows
of the hills and valleys
of this battlefield land
catching its breath
exhausting the wind in the weather
by the sway of the grasses
and the movements of sage
those naked bodies
fallen and lingering and fading to bone
like leaf-stripped forests
as a naked lamentation
of mortal flesh gone still
once quilled with arrows
rooted in the red sorrow
of surrendered life
what slows the heart here
where watches live on for stolen hours
by ticks and twitches
is an old and ancient annihilation
of us all
these *Custer's men*
who, from the wrong side of darkness
come to nothing
where the value of dying
is measured
in pierced-money medallions
and the worthlessness
of dead flesh
by what compass point

might we then seek true north
in the quivering jelly
of a black needle shivering under glass
who then dials the direction of loss
while the Little Bighorn River
lay its path like a stripped vein
where the only truth is water
while this thirsting of ghosts
drinks deep from the blue withholding of rain

Heyoka – the contrarian

it seems there is a fine line
between madness and divinity
a holy man may well simply be *unsound of mind*
his visions partaking in chaos
and that fine distinction
between the lunatic and the knave
is a thin lacuna
an otiose whisp of invisible air
a vapid trace of mist
like arrows of fog
with tips of light that pierce the wing
and swirl away
in feather drift like wind-blown smoke
the fruit that falls in darkness from the bough
mere odor and the weightless perfume
of cider rising through aromas of the night

consider the Heyoka of the Sioux
the contrarian
who speaks with the gods of thunder
the joker riding backwards into battle
singing on his pony
with a quiver in his voice
oh, how he clowns and fools
and jukes and all the widdershins weapons
with his bow plucked and loosed
at the blue adversary of a clear sky

as though the sun were an enemy breast
and the moon
a touchable skull
a stone-clubbed rival
contending with the stars

I too am impossibly foolish
footsteps in water mark my way
a pebble daps its halo waves
a circle plunges and subsides
this path I follow
follows me
in radiant vanishments
of ephemeral events
that shoal the sand in cloudy beds

I disappear in shouldering of combers coming in
the blue loom of a second sky receives my body
like the dross and dust my breath become a winnowing of rain

My Lands

the great Sioux warrior Crazy Horse
prophesied that in the future
long after his death
he would return to the earth
his image fixed in stone—
and so
his face emerges
as from a whispering veil of rock
a visage looming over the landscape
from the summit
of Thunder Mountain
no photographer
ever captured his soul
no pen
ever shaped his hand

like Caesar
he was slain
his body betrayed
gored from behind by a trooper's bayonet
his bones
lost to time
lie buried in the mystery of dust

oh Badlands, oh Black Hills
ancestor granite
feldspar-fathered host
and all who pray by the spirit
of horses
by this élan vital
revealed in light

each year
the sculptors blast
and cut
and loosening so the scree
might yield
a gesture, surrender a single hand
bequeath an arm
as Moses in memoriam
might glimpse again
a milk-and-honey land
remorseful of his sight
and there
a horse unborn
Homeric in the voice of winds
from wooden Troy
like weather in the pines
the heartbeat
of a hammer breaking at the breast
as by the blood of ghosts
and by the phantoms of the flesh
some revenant erosion blooms
like a river song
a shoulder rising from a wave
a breath of broken open sky

"my lands are where my dead are buried"
he said as though
his granite gaze weren't blind

Wishtonwish
and the Barking Squirrel

I was looking
at the hawk sorrow
of a prairie dog town
all those mounded holes
perforating the earth
poked over that subterranean warren
that colony of singers
barking my presence
with even a privy place
caved in a hollow room
for the hard reminder
of a rodent's final concern
with the pebbled remnants
of an organized latrine
and also
the sleep chambers
where small dreams
slow the breath
of these busy-boned creatures
rising out and running loose in useless freedom
like the broken-away teeth of well-thumbed comb

how the God who made horses
and then gave the wind away
to the grass and the bison thunder
of this sad land
kept faith in what was mostly
an underlife, like root work
gone deep after water
in the moiling for moisture
of the rarity of rain
and there in the shallow shadow brooding
of a wing span
in the swift and ephemeral darkness
like dust whirling where words subside
like water come touching outward
as when you overfill a vase

Ode on Devil's Tower
South Dakota

"the guide kept telling us how this sacred site
was where Spielberg filmed the closing scene
in *Close Encounters of the Third Kind*"

how might Devil's Tower
shed
the impoverishment
of Hollywood's trivial dream
oh how it suffers from
the glamorous veneer
of glowing lights
and the awful swirl of
recent fame
in the alienated universe
see where
the lonesomeness of bear-clawed stone
rises
how the snake-climbed face of rock
slithers upward
scarred by myth smoking over
like mist—the ursine monument
a stone's reminder
of constellations
fallen at the heels
where heaven slums
with all the ambient invisibility
of galaxies dimmed to nothing
emptied out like milk sour
too long warm
what a curdled firmament
washed with lumps of yellow-white
like words that sting the tongue
how then

reclaim these altitudes
these sacred heights
when wonder fades away
like old cathedrals
when their fonts are dry
as water
dries from where it's splashed
on sun-scorched rock

I hear a cell phone ring
two voices
and a third
one volume in the overlay
soaks in
like watercoloured gesso
staining where the canvas
fakes the sky

all art is artificial
to an undiscerning eye

A Staying Place

today I found myself wondering
what the word *home*
might mean to the wanderers of the world
those nomadic people
who pick up and move
as the wind moves
through the meadow
or as sand drifts on a dune
the tinkers of Ireland
the Romani of Europe
the Lakota of the west
the Bedu of the desert
how they follow the wadi
the coulee, the valley's green ease
where are the better ways through the badlands
for the water that shallows
over the earth
in a dry season
of evaporate light

what does it mean to be homesick
to those who find the romance of meandering
where the pines darken the glade
with bark that smells of butterscotch
and vanilla
in the *sun softened* light
releasing its flavour and perfume
for that vagabond heart
of the gypsy in motion

like appaloosas on the plains
and the cloud ghost
of a dark shape
where a shadow touches the surface of the land
like the cooling of desire
in a blush of flesh after loving

well as for me I was born
as a tree is born, rooted in its own
breeze-dappled chiaroscuro
fallen five generations below the waterline
where the well runs deep
as an unseen sorrow

and in the bird seeding of some fertile and far away
place I linger and move linger and move
and the wonder of home
crosses the great fever of long water
the land bridge no longer there
the graves of my people
marked in stone
called a staying place

Fourteen Variations on *Wild*

there
in the longing
of an open palm

wild seed calms the sparrow

*

the plough
that tames the land
also turns the horses

*

he who rides
the I-beam into blue

falls twice

*

consider the lilies
how they toiled
in Eden

*

the dead bird proves
the presence of a window
finding stillness in the glass

*

sometimes it seems
my soul's
the songbird of an empty cage

*

when once upon a time
weeds were grown-wild roses
their red thorns clawed
the crimson skies of dawn

*

here where mile-deep ice
went calving backwards
lo those many summers
on the lakes of time

*

oh, how I've come
to hate the word *lifestyle*
living as I do
in a lawned-over world

*

you ask of me "how old is the number 2?"

I don't know
though I'm quite certain
it's older than
the number 3

*

oh my disobedient shadow
wild companion
to the lightless dark

when the bluecoats came to the black hills of Dakota
intent upon killing the wives and children of the Lakota

at day's end the widow sorrow
of each soldier's wife
took up its pen

*

there are fields somewhere
of the farm at home
where the grass is greener
on the other side of absent fences

*

in this battle
of cultures – which
side are you on ...

well, as for me, I assure you
I'm on the inside

If I Were to Live
Where the Soil
is Worn Away

if I were to live
where the soil is worn away
by walking
like windswept sand
or runnels
where the water flows
above the land
who then
might trace the spirit
in the stone
limb shadows
cool the earth
to shape a path of orchard light
how generations
wear away like wheel ruts
moving through the wheat
or trails
that crush the green
and bend
the seed's result
as proof of passing
there the ghost of grass
and there
the smile lines
of a solemn vow
upon the bones of time

oh look
where life has creased the palm
or cracked a sorrow shell
within a printed face of rock
the fragile moment
of a momentary veil of mist
the catcher's net
upon a wave
the shaded crosshatch
sinks into the swell
where like an inbreath
promissory words become a prayer

see how the trace of footfalls
burn with vivid rumours
of the past
like the breath that bends
the flickering of altar flame
the way the voice remains aloft
while candles cling to wicks of temporary light

Jokers Wild

would I ever have thought it
as a child
that one day in the recent past
of a once-upon-a-time
distant future since then
that I would stand
at the graveyard gate
where the green surmise
of the wild west
would bury the dead man's hand
till the bones came out through the glove
like roots that grow in search of water
all aces and eights
and the residue
of a bad luck day
come smouldering up
and out of the earth
like the burning off of late-spring frost
the kind I've seen so often
like gun smoke in the breast
near the breath of broken fences
and that greying over the land
of spirit memory
from the season of fame in youth
even the names
Wild Bill Hickock and
the drunken slur of Calamity Jane
rattle the tongue in the chain drag
of consonants that level away American legends

oh I was once
cowboy Johnny
riding a cockhorse broom
until time gave way
to the weight of apples
and blossoms, blossoms and
apples again
in that perseverating orchard
on the farm of my childhood
under blue-sky sour-cherry dark-pit heavens

and there in Deadwood
there at the cutting edge of forever
with fifty-two jesters to the pack
I played the card-counter's awful lament
having learned since those sugar-foot days
since those halcyon days

that certain indecisive creatures
after crawling ashore
turned their backs to the land
having changed their minds
about breathing

Orpheus in the Badlands
of South Dakota

the sunlight in the badlands
goes seeking
the snake to rattle
that infant serpent
sunning himself
in among the hoodoo spools
of eroded stone
slipping like a venomous rope
out of the bowels
of mud-brown rock
that fanged reminder
of the unloved
gut-length of lost Eden
hissing and fork-tongued
dropping his shade
like the hanged weight
of a death-measured
execution
the banal hawser of original sin
and the drift breath
of flute music
come to silence
that outdistances beauty
in the echo shadow
of inaudible life
and there he waits
as a resolute and
ineluctable warning
the dark thread of spilled water
splashed in a dry place
the surreal mirage of arroyos
that once were rivers
and bones with voices lifting out of the earth
like the little twists of wind that barely raise the dust

Ten-Thousand-Year-Old
Pictographs

not far from where
the multi-coloured hills
have lain their turquoise gels
against the sun
some ancient artist
stained the arching vaults
within a cave
those pictographs preserved on stone
like dreams
that fade away from bone
or clouds
that whisper misty horsetails
on the wind
the human urgency of ice
that shapes a lake
that moves the land
as rivers carve old canyons
where they were
in vanishing arroyos over time
like the words that guide
the poet's hand
across the vacant page
in cursive sentience
emergent from the blank intelligence of white
gone backwards
through the smoke
that marks the fire with a smudge
like blushing of desire in a veil

Three Days
to Bury the Horses

… for Mary Ann Mulhern

"You need to remember that it took 3 days just to bury the horses"
… a history teacher's comment
on the aftermath of the Battle of Gettysburg

today as I cycled through smoke
on my way to the gym
inhaling the wildfire particulate
hazing the smouldering air
come here from the eye-blink of the burning woods
of the far-away boreal forest
perhaps thinking of winters
at the cottage
or evenings round a campfire
in the summer swarms
of malarial songs and the cry of the loon
and the baying of coyotes
in the bloodthirsty out-of-door's gloaming
I also thought of myself
as an essentially silly boy
in the basement of my friend Raymond's house
drawing fire through cedar
and watching it glow at the lit end
choking on kindling
and dreaming of being an adult
in a movie
sucking on the romantic cigarette
across the fluted glass from a willing debutante
or as a young university buck scorching my lungs
with hashish on a pin

or the snap and crackle of a roll-your-own joint
with the zig-zag logo on the table
meanwhile my favourite singer, Beatle Paul
remembers smoking English tea
in his father's pipe
with John Lennon as a co-conspirator
like my pals with corn silk shrinking backwards
into the green ache of a light-headed sickness

and so it seems to me
it's little wonder that we humans *war*
burning this candle of words
both ways from the middle
and waiting for the darkness
taking three days to bury the horses

Visiting Mount Rushmore
on a Glorious
Morning in May

I look up
having come north by
northwest
to view the surreal image
of this quartet
of stone-faced presidents
and I confess
that what fascinated me most
having rounded
the tourist trail
rising and wending
through the well-groomed overgrowth
that catch-breath
climb as I walk
widdershins, having heard
by rumour
in the aftermath of trekking
that there was
more ease to the east
of the mountain
and I looked up
as though
I were sleeping
under the dream ceiling
of an ever-expanding
overarching canopy of blue stars blooming
and there *they* were
appearing before me
the four carved physiognomies
of human gods

like the death masks of famous men
with high foreheads
no longer breathing
behind the lime-and-water
with a great drying away of the spirit in the bones

and I swear
it was the grey glint of shadow
cast by Teddy Roosevelt's pince nez
the dark flash of absent glass
a trick of the light on the rock
like the trompe-l'oeil
of a ghost's mind thinking
'do you see what I see'

An Afterword from the Publisher, Richard M. Grove

After reading, pondering and enjoying this little, but not so trivial, contribution to CanLit I decided to propose this afterword to John. We agreed that I should place it here at the end of the book. The first thing that I wanted to comment on was the title. I found it to be a fitting and poignant choice, reflecting the author's introspection on the enduring legacy of history, culture, and memory tied to iconic and sacred sites in America's West. Each poem questions the established narratives of famous historical moments and individuals, asking readers to reconsider the ideas of heroism, conquest, and cultural significance through a deeply reflective lens. The poems explore the legacy of battles, the monumental figures associated with them, and the contrasting cultural values held by Indigenous and European settler societies.

In the eponymous poem, *The Last Stand*, the imagery of Custer's defeat at Little Bighorn is starkly subverted. Rather than glorifying a final heroic stand, the poem presents a scene where:

> *there was no last stand*
> *it was rather*
> *a scattering of bones*
> *like the wild and random*
> *aftermath*
> *of a wind-torn orchard.*

This scattering of bones is a haunting picture of defeat, a moment where idealized visions of heroism fall away, leaving only remnants—a "vaporous absence" of a romanticized narrative. The title *The Last Stand* echoes this subversion, pushing readers to question which perspective is dominant in the historical accounts we remember and whose "stand" we choose to memorialize.

The title of the book further speaks to the complex heritage of the land itself, as demonstrated in the poem "Upon Visiting the Battlefield at Little Bighorn River." Here, the battlefield serves as a:

> *naked lamentation*
> *of mortal flesh gone still,*

and the markers of those who died are portrayed as ghostly imprints against the landscape:

> *white markers*
> *milkening the swells and hollows*
> *of the hills and valleys.*

The title's question reverberates here, as it evokes the ghosts of soldiers and Indigenous warriors alike. Rather than celebrating one over the other, the poem underscores a universal mortality, asking readers to consider what any of us gain from war and what legacies we inherit from these losses.

In his preface, John recounts his own pilgrimage to sites like the Crazy Horse Memorial and Mount Rushmore, exploring the contrast between the romanticized images we've constructed and the deep, often somber, truths that lie beneath. He notes, "Hollywood has corrupted the meaning of Mount Rushmore. ... I wanted to claw back the false mask of cinematic glamour to reveal the original myth of the bear claw ascent of the rock." It seems to me that this desire to strip away the pretence imposed by modern society resonates with the title of the collection.

Even though the poem "Heyoka – the contrarian" took a few ponderous readings, for me it seems to align well with the collections title, *The Last Stand*. I found that it illustrates a form of defiance that is both profound and unconventional. The Heyoka, a sacred clown in Sioux culture, embodies resistance by performing actions in reverse, challenging norms, and unsettling expectations. The clown's contrary stance somehow reflects the theme of defying conventional ideas about conflict, victory, and legacy in a beautifully paradoxical way.

It became evident that the poem captures this idea of unconventional defiance through the Heyoka's backward actions, embodying a somewhat absurd form of resistance. Lines like:

> *the joker riding backwards into battle*
> *singing on his pony*
> *with a quiver in his voice*

emphasize the Heyoka's approach to conflict, inverting traditional warrior imagery and creating an unsettling yet profound impact. The lines:

> *with his bow plucked and loosed*
> *at the blue adversary of a clear sky*
> *as though the sun were an enemy breast*

seem to further illustrate his defiance against conventional targets, resisting typical ideas of battle and legacy.

These vivid images show that the Heyoka's stand, though seemingly foolish, challenges the audience to see beyond traditional bravery, aligning with the title *The Last Stand* as a meditation on profound yet unconventional defiance.

Ultimately, the title of the book, *The Last Stand* encapsulates a collection that reflects on lost histories, cultural erasure, and the cost of mythologizing certain events while disregarding others. The title itself becomes a reminder that the narratives we uphold as significant—whether of Custer, Crazy Horse, or countless unnamed Indigenous people—depend on perspective. The author's journey through America's West is both a literal and figurative attempt to "claw back" to an honest retelling, one that acknowledges multiple narratives and recognizes the "last stands" of various groups whose stories are equally deserving of reverence and reflection.

There are many stunning lines and provocative poems in this collection. I would suggest you read this collection stone sober sitting up on a hard kitchen chair. There is nothing warm and romantic about this collection that would make you want to recline with a comfy blanket over your lap. It is a good thing that the book is short because you will want to read it over and over again to grasp the full intensity of each stunning line.

I hope you enjoy the poetic profundities of John B. Lee as much as I do.

Richard Grove,
Writer, Editor, Publisher

A Short Bio Note on the Author

In 2005 John B. Lee was inducted as Poet Laureate of Brantford and in 2015 he was appointed Honourary Poet Laureate of Norfolk County. A recipient of over eighty prestigious international awards for his writing, he has well-over seventy books published to date and is the editor of nine anthologies. Called "the greatest living poet in English," by poet George Whipple, his most recent book, *Stronger in Broken Places*, was published by Aeolus House in 2024. He lives with wife Cathy in a lake house overlooking Long Point Bay, in Port Dover, Ontario where he works as a full-time author.

www.ingramcontent.com/pod-product-compliance
Lightning Source LLC
Chambersburg PA
CBHW030526130626
46549CB00007B/3118